W9-CNA-360

25 Fun Things to Do
OUTSIDE

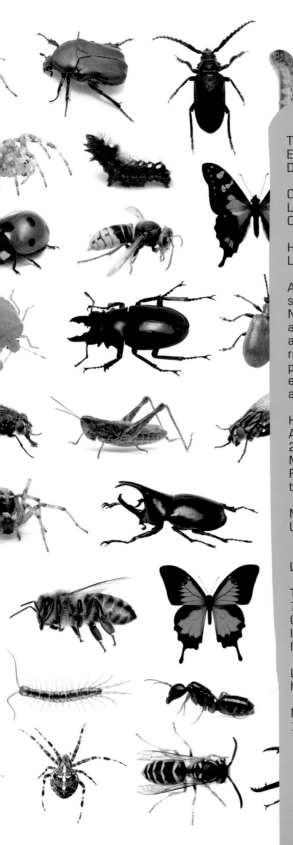

Thanks to the creative team:
Editor: Tim Harris
Design: Perfect Bound Ltd

Hungry Tomato®
A division of Lerner Publishing Group, Inc.
241 First Avenue North
Minneapolis, MN 55401 USA
For reading levels and more information, look up this title at www.lernerbooks.com.

Main body text set in
URW Dock regular.

Library of Congress Cataloging-in-Publication Data

The Cataloging-in-Publication Data for *25 Fun Things to Do Outside* is on file at the Library of Congress.
ISBN 978-1-5415-0131-7 (lib. bdg.)
ISBN 978-1-5415-4274-7 (eb pdf)

LC record available at
https://lccn.loc.gov/2018034054

Manufactured in the United States of America
1-43801-33647-10/2/2018

25 Fun Things to Do
OUTSIDE

PAUL MASON

HUNGRY
TOMATO™

MINNEAPOLIS

CONTENTS

Get Outdoors!

Some days—like when you're sick, or the rain is pouring down—you just don't want to go out. If you CAN get outside, though, it's a really good idea to go. These are just some of the reasons why:

1 You need sunlight. *Too much sunlight is harmful, but everyone needs a little. Sunshine causes your body to produce vitamin D, which helps you get chemicals called calcium and phosphate from food. These make bones, teeth, and muscles grow strong.*

2 Being outside might make you see better. *One scientific report says that for every hour you play outside, you are 2 percent less likely to need glasses.*

3 Being active makes you smarter. *Being outside usually means you are being active. For example, you might decide to go for a hike, build a shelter, or go on a hunt to photograph wildlife.*
   Several investigations have shown that students who get physically fit usually start to get better grades:
- *Their memories improve*
- *Their brains start to make connections in new ways*
- *They can concentrate better*

4 Being outside makes good friends. *When you and your friends do challenges such as camping out, or even fun, simple things like going for a picnic, it makes your friendships stronger. It also helps you learn how to work with others.*

SAFETY OUTSIDE

Part of the fun of being outside can be getting away from grown-ups. This is fine—as long as your grown-ups:
- *know where you are*
- *have said it's OK*

STAYING IN IS NOT AN OPTION

Staying indoors and gaming is fun—but it won't accomplish many of these things.

1. Camp Out

Camping with your friends is a great adventure. Plan ahead (and check the weather forecast) and you will still be talking about the campout years later.

THINGS YOU DEFINITELY NEED:

- Sleep mat
- Sleeping bag
- A drink
- A light

THINGS YOU MIGHT LIKE:

- A warm, dry night
- Food
- Bug spray
- Pillow
- Tent

1 **Pick a place.** Your campsite needs to be somewhere level that is easy to get to and is safe. Lots of kids do their first campout in a backyard.*

2 **Clear the ground.** Check the ground for stones, sticks, and anything else that might keep you awake.

3 **Enjoy being outdoors.** Just because there's no TV or internet doesn't mean there is nothing to do except go to sleep. Try building a campfire, like on page 7, and roasting some marshmallows.

4 **Get some z's.** When everyone's tired, climb into your sleeping bags and (if you forgot one) wish you had a pillow. Don't worry, though. You will get to sleep.

5 **Do a cleanup.** Everyone will probably wake up as soon as it gets light. Check the campsite for trash—if there is any, pick it up.

If you are sleeping in a tent, make sure there is nothing sharp that could stick up through the floor.

Stick together—but if your friend snores, bring earplugs!

CAMPING SAFETY

Always check everyone's parents think the place you have picked is safe for camping out. Make sure you have permission to sleep there, too.

*Make a pact not to chicken out later and go indoors!

2. Build a Campfire

TOP TIP: make sure there's room to get a match to the kindling!

Campfires are great for talking around, toasting food, and keeping warm, so knowing how to make one is a useful skill.

1 **Find a fire site.** Your fire needs to be at least 2 yards from anything that could catch fire. Build a ring of big rocks to stop the fire from spreading.

2 **Build a fire.** In the middle goes the kindling: dry leaves and grass, which catch fire easily. Then add the twigs and a few larger sticks.

3 **Light the fire.** Light the kindling. If you light one edge and blow on it, the flame should spread—but don't stay close for too long.

FIRE SAFETY

Never build a campfire if there is a fire ban, or where there is a risk of wildfires.

ALL YOU NEED

- Big rocks
- Dry leaves, grass, twigs, larger sticks, and small logs
- Matches

The ring should be about half a yard across.

3. Find Orion

Orion is one of the most famous star constellations. It can be seen in the night sky from anywhere in the world.

1 **Look for Orion's belt.** Orion the Hunter's belt is made of three bright stars close together in a line.

2 **Find his shoulders and knees.** Above and below Orion's belt (but further apart), look for four more bright stars.

3 **Look for Orion's sword.** Between Orion's belt and knees are three more stars, close together. In the middle is the Orion Nebula, a place where stars are born.

4 **Find the rest of Orion.** Now you have the basic shape, you can pick out the rest of the stars that make Orion and his bow.

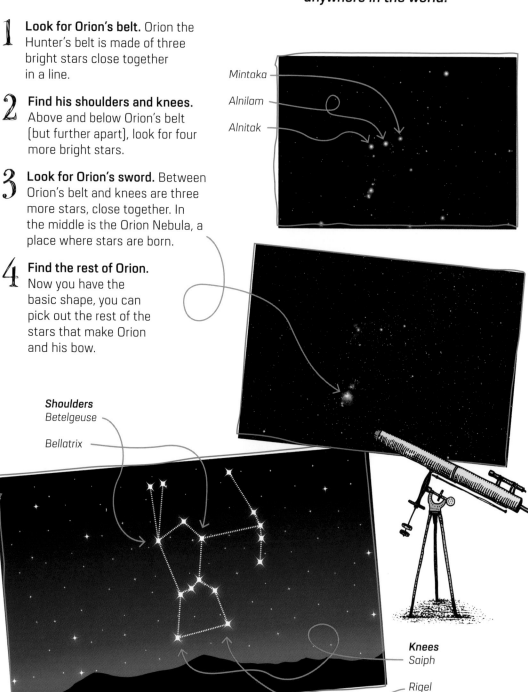

Mintaka

Alnilam

Alnitak

Shoulders
Betelgeuse

Bellatrix

Knees
Saiph

Rigel

4. Go on a Hike

Going on a hike means walking somewhere—usually to a place further away than you would normally walk.

1 **Pick a route.** Decide where to go. Short hikes, about 2–3 miles long, are good for beginners.

2 **Work out your timing.** Most people can walk at about 3 mph, so a 6 mile hike will take 2–3 hours, including stops.

Take water to drink, and on hikes of more than 2 hours take food too.

3 **Gather your gear.** Check the weather forecast and decide whether to put rain gear, warm clothes, sunscreen, etc. in your backpack.

4 **Go hiking.** Stick to your route, stop when you are tired or see something interesting, and enjoy being outside!

ALL YOU NEED

- Comfortable shoes
- Backpack
- Drink and food

ROUTE NOTES

Tell an adult your route and when you will be back. Then they will know if you're late and where to look for you.

5. Go on a Trash Pickup

Plastic trash can stay around for years. It looks terrible and harms animals and plants. Help your beach or park become plastic-free!

ADVANCE PLANNING

Check with the local council or beach owner to check:
a) that the pickup is allowed
b) what you should do with the plastic

ALL YOU NEED

- Volunteers
- Garbage bags
- Gloves to protect your hands

1 **Advertise!** Tell your friends, the school council, and your local newspaper the time and date of the trash pickup.

2 **Organize teams.** Have someone responsible in charge of teams of three. Each team picks up all the plastic in its area.

3 **Sort the plastic.** Each team uses two garbage bags to separate recyclable and non-recyclable plastic.

4 **Tidy up.** Recycle what you can and dump the rest of the waste in the trash.

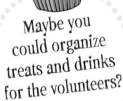

Maybe you could organize treats and drinks for the volunteers?

6. Play a Game of Cat Attack

This is a great game for people of any age—as long as they aren't scared of a bit of water.

1 **Fill the balloons.** Draw bird faces on the balloons, fill them with water, and put them in the bucket.

2 **Chalk up some cats.** Draw some cat faces on the ground with chalk.
Big cat faces = 1 point
Smaller faces = 2 points
Tiny faces = 3 points

3 **Attack!** From behind a chalk line, take turns lobbing balloons at the cats. If you wipe one out, you get the points.

4 **Clean up.** Once all the cats are gone, pick up the burst balloons and brush away any leftover chalk.

ALL YOU NEED
- Wash-away chalk
- Water balloons
- Marker
- Bucket

7. Take your Friends on a Treasure Hunt

ALL YOU NEED

- A compass
- A notepad and pencil
- White paper and colored pencils
- Old coffee or tea leaves
- Treasure

This activity is in two parts. First, make a treasure map for your friends to follow. Then you hide the treasure and they try to find it.

1 **Find a hiding place.** Find somewhere to hide the treasure. It could be under some bushes, up a tree, or buried in a hole.

2 **Work out a route.** Now work out a route from there to the starting place. It should be as confusing as possible! Go around buildings and over obstacles.

3 **Count it out.** Retrace your route back to the treasure spot. Count the direction and number of steps from one stop to another. Note everything on the notepad.

4 **Draw the map.** Draw out the route carefully, in pencil at first. Add directions like: "Walk 15 steps due east," or "After 21 steps, turn north between two trees."

5 **Make the map look old.** Rub the map with old coffee or tea, then leave it to dry in the sun. Rip the edges and scrunch it up.

6 **Hide your treasure.** Your treasure chest could be a tin with some cookies, a candy bar, or a sandwich for lunch. Don't make it anything too valuable, in case someone else finds it!

7 **Set your friends on the treasure-hunt challenge.** They could do it together, or one at a time (in which case the person who finds the treasure in the least time wins it).

8. Go on a Bug Safari

ALL YOU NEED

- Sheet of paper
- Clipboard
- Pen
- Possibly a magnifying glass or digital camera

You don't have to go to Africa to go on safari—not if it's a bug safari. A backyard or park is all that's required.

1 **Draw a grid.** Name the things you expect to find (you could draw them too). Leave space for unexpected bugs!

2 **Start hunting.** Now start looking for bugs. Some might be flying. Others will be under rocks, on leaves, or beneath bushes.

3 **Add it all up.** Add up what you find. Are some bugs more common than others? What size are they? Why might there be more of these?

Every time you see a bug, add a mark to your grid. You could take a photo too.

9. Organize a Night Hike

At night, outdoor smells and noises are different. Familiar routes no longer look the same.

1 **Set a meeting place.** Tell everyone where to meet and when. As they arrive, put their names on a list.

2 **Stick together.** On the hike, make sure the group doesn't get separated. One person leads the way. Someone else brings up the rear and calls out if the leaders get too far ahead.

3 **Stop and listen.** Once in a while you should stop, turn off your flashlights, and listen. Everything sounds louder (and more creepy!) in the dark.

4 **Check everyone back in.** When you get back, check off people's names on the list to make sure no one has been left behind.

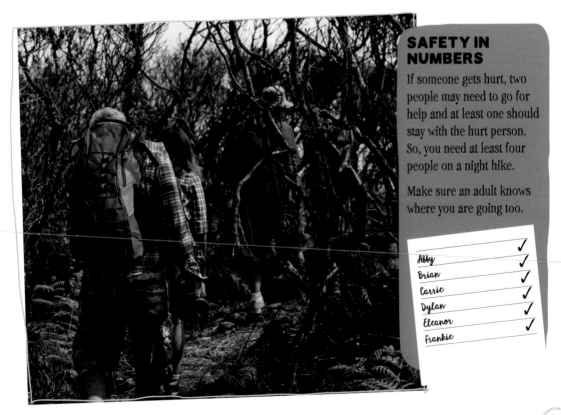

SAFETY IN NUMBERS

If someone gets hurt, two people may need to go for help and at least one should stay with the hurt person. So, you need at least four people on a night hike.

Make sure an adult knows where you are going too.

Abby	✓
Brian	✓
Carrie	✓
Dylan	✓
Eleanor	✓
Frankie	

10. Fix a Puncture

Imagine: you're going out for a ride with your friends in an hour, but when you get to your bike—argh! Flat tire! Here's what to do:

1 **Remove the wheel.** Many bikes have a quick-release lever for this, but you might need to use a tool called a spanner.

2 **Remove one side of the tire.** Use your tire levers to lift one side of the tire off the wheel. The first bit is tricky, but then it gets easier.

3 **Lift off the other side.** Repeat the process, but lever the other side of the tire off in the same direction as before.

You have now removed the tire and the inner tube inside it.

4 **Find the puncture.** Pull the inner tube out of the tire. Pump up the inner tube. You'll hear a little hiss of air where the puncture is, and can mark it with the chalk.

5 **Check the tire.** Check the tire to see if a thorn or sharp rock is sticking through anywhere. If it is, take it out, or the inner tube will get another puncture.

6 **Patch the puncture.** Use the sandpaper to roughen the tube and then stick the repair patch carefully over the puncture. Press down hard, then add a little air to the tube—just enough to make it round.

7 **Tuck in the inner tube.** Put the inner tube back inside the tire.

8 **Put the tire back on the wheel.** Start by putting the valve through the valve hole. Then push one side of the tire into place over the edge of the wheel. Slowly work around—you might need to use the levers for the last bit.

9 **Check the tube and finish.** Make sure the tube is properly inside the tire. If it is, push the other side of the tire onto the wheel.

You might have to use your tire levers for the last bit.

10 **Pump up and go!** Pump up the tire as hard as you can, which will help keep the patch in place. Put the wheel back on your bike, and go and meet your friends.

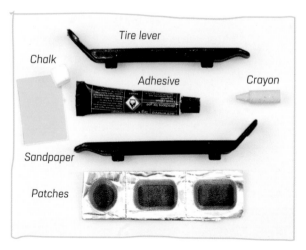

Tire lever

Chalk

Adhesive

Crayon

Sandpaper

Patches

1

Unscrew the valve
to pump air into
the tube

2

3

4

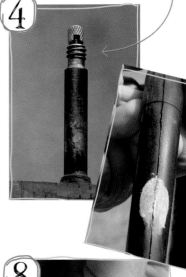

6

8

17

11. Learn to Yodel

A yodel is a loud sound using the natural break between your normal voice and a high-pitched version of it.

1 **Find the yodel break.** Start singing "Ohhhhhhh" as low as you can. Keep getting higher until you hear the break.

2 **Practice.** Keep going back and forth between the two versions of your voice. You can try to use different sounds.

3 **Sing a yodel!** Most yodels use one low note and two high ones. Try out this cowboy yodel:
   'Yodel *ay* (low), *ee* (high) *dee* (high)'.

Yodeling was originally used in the Alps to communicate across the mountains. It eventually became popular with cowboy singers.

12. Play "She'll be Comin' 'Round the Mountain"
on a Ukulele

1 **Learn these chords**. You can play "She'll be Comin' 'Round the Mountain" with five simple chords. To play the chords, run your thumb down the strings from top to bottom. This is called strumming.

Maybe on your campout (see page 6) you'd like to sing a few songs? Here is a simple one to practice on the ukulele before you go.

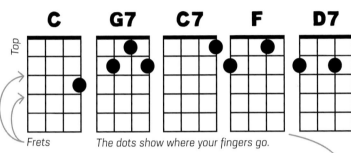

Top

C   **G7**   **C7**   **F**   **D7**

Frets   *The dots show where your fingers go.*

2 **Add the chords to the song**. At first, just play the chords when the song says. When you get more confident, you can add some extra strums.

ALL YOU NEED

• A ukulele (really, that's it)

Chorus

       C
She'll be coming 'round the mountain

when she comes

She'll be coming 'round the mountain
       G7
when she comes
      C   **C7**
She'll be coming 'round the mountain,
     F   **D7**
She'll be coming 'round the mountain,
      C   **G7**
She'll be coming 'round the mountain
      C
when she comes

Verse

She'll be driving six white horses when she comes
She'll be driving six white horses when she comes
She'll be driving six white horses,
She'll be driving six white horses,
She'll be driving six white horses when she comes.

13. Paint like Pollock

ALL YOU NEED

- Big sheet of paper
- Bigger sheets of cardboard
- Paints with different colors
- One paintbrush per color

Jackson Pollock is a famous artist. He uses splashes and drops of color to make bright, many-layered paintings.

1 **Lay out your paper.** Put it on the ground, right in the middle of the big pieces of cardboard.

2 **Add one color.** Load up your brush, then flick the paint onto the paper.* Flicking at different heights and strengths will give different effects.

3 **Add more colors.** Keep adding colors until the painting looks just right to you.

Make sure you are wearing old clothes you don't mind staining.

14. Make a Rock Stack Sculpture

These sculptures look great anywhere—what's really fun is to build one, then leave it for other people to enjoy.

1 **Find some rocks.** Flat rocks are usually best. You will need a mixture of sizes.

2 **Work out how they fit together.** The biggest rocks usually go at the bottom.

3 **Check each layer for balance.** Make sure each layer is solidly balanced on the one underneath. You don't want your sculpture to blow over in the wind!

ALL YOU NEED
- Different-sized rocks
- Patience

15. Make a Pinecone Bird Feeder

A bird feeder is a sure way to attract birds. In winter, it might even help them stay alive.

ALL YOU NEED

- Pinecones (dried out so they don't open)
- Suet or lard
- Bird seed
- Raisins
- Peanuts
- Grated cheese
- A mixing bowl
- Scissors
- String

1 **Mix it up.** Chop the suet or lard into small pieces and mix with the other ingredients. Use your fingers to squish it all together.

2 **Make a cone ball.** Put three or four pinecones together and bind them up with string. Leave about 20 inches of string.

3 **Add the food.** Press the food onto the cone ball, covering it completely.

4 **Hang the feeder.** Tie the loose end of the string to a branch, fence, or railing. Hungry birds will soon start to arrive.

16. Photograph Birds

Now that you have a bird feeder (see page 22), you have a great chance to become a wildlife photographer.

1 **Line up your shot.** Decide the best angle to take the photo from. Avoid looking toward the sun.

2 **Hide yourself.** Hide in a nearby building if there is one. If not, maybe you could put up a tent or build yourself a shelter like the one on page 24.

3 **Be patient.** Try to keep still as you wait for the birds to arrive. They will not approach if you are wriggling about or making a noise.

MAKE A NATURE ALBUM

Once you have photos of different birds, you could put together a nature notebook with facts about what you have seen.

1 Research your birds. First, you need to know which birds you photographed. Find out by asking people, looking in books in the library, and researching on the internet.

2 Add some facts. Now organize what you know. Each photograph might have an entry like this:

> Name: House sparrow
> Male/female: male
> When photographed: May 2018
> Place: northern Georgia
> Behavior: fast-moving, gathering as much food as possible (to feed chicks?)

3 Put together an album. You could do this by printing everything and sticking it down in a notebook. Or you could make an online album.

17. Build a Forest Shelter

Whether you are outside in the day or camping out at night, a shelter comes in handy. It can shield you from rain, wind, and hot sunshine.

ALL YOU NEED

- Two trees close together
- One long, straight, fallen branch
- Lots of thick sticks
- Two 3-yard lengths of rope or strong cord
- Branches with leaves

1 **Assemble your branches.** The long branch should be a bit longer than the gap between the two trees. The thick sticks should be at least 1.5 yards long.

2 **Tie on the long branch.** Tie the long branch to the trees so that it is parallel to the ground about 1 yard up.

3 **Lay down the thick sticks.** Now lean the thick sticks against the long branch. The longer they are, the more space there will be under your shelter.

PERMISSION

If you are gathering wood for a shelter, make sure you have permission from the landowner:
a) to be on the land
b) to collect wood

4 **Add leafy branches.** Try to find branches that have fallen but still have leaves. Lay these on the outer side of your wall.

5 **Install a bed.** The last thing to do is make the shelter comfortable. Gather together soft, dry leaves and make a thick bed of them under the roof.

Ideally the sticks should be no more than 45° from the ground. An angle of 30° will give you more room, but you will need longer sticks.

30°
45°

If you can only find one tree in the right place, build a sloping shelter like this.

WHICH DIRECTION?

If your shelter is to hide from wind and rain, find two trees that are across the direction the wind is coming from.

If your shelter is for shade, find trees linked by an imaginary east-west line. Your shelter will give most shade if it faces north (north of the Equator) or south (south of the Equator). You can find north using a watch with hands:

North of the Equator, turn the watch until the hour hand points directly at the sun. Now imagine a line halfway between the 12 on the watch face and the hour hand. That line points south, so north is the opposite way.

South of the Equator, point the 12 on the watch face at the sun; north is halfway between the 12 and the hour hand.

N

N

18. Go for a Picnic

ALL YOU NEED

- Bread
- Cheese
- Lunch meat
- Salt and mayonnaise
- Something to drink
- Knife
- Picnic blanket

People often say food tastes better outdoors. Going for a simple picnic with your family or friends is a good way to find out.

1 **Pick a picnic spot.** Remember you have to carry your picnic stuff, so somewhere a long way off might not be ideal.

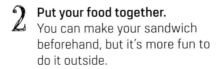

2 **Put your food together.** You can make your sandwich beforehand, but it's more fun to do it outside.

3 **Pack in, pack out.** Once the picnic is over, check your spot to make sure you have left no garbage behind.

Lay slices of cheese and then meat on the bread. Sprinkle on a teeny bit of salt, then a thin layer of mayonnaise.

19. Cook Potatoes on a Campfire

If you build a campfire (see page 7) and feel hungry, why not use the fire's heat to bake some potatoes?

(see page 7)

ALL YOU NEED
- Medium-sized potatoes
- Tinfoil
- Butter and salt
- Knife

1 Preparation. Prepare the potatoes by pricking the surface all over, then cutting them in half. Put butter and a tiny bit of salt in the middle, press the halves together and wrap them in tinfoil.

2 Place the potatoes. Not right in the fire! *

3 Wait . . . then eat. Normal potatoes take at least 45 minutes to cook. Sweet potatoes take half as long.

*Rake some red-hot coals to the edge of the fire. Put the potatoes on them, then rake more coals over the top. Repeat as the coals cool down.

20. Go Crabbing

Crabbing—catching crabs by dangling bait—is a fun way to spend time at the seaside.

ALL YOU NEED

- String or handline
- Bucket
- Small fishing net
- Small mesh bag
- Bait (crabs like fish)

1 **Prepare the bucket.** Put seawater in the bucket, plus seaweed and pebbles. This makes it more like the crab's normal surroundings.

2 **Bait up.** Put your bait inside the small mesh bag and tie it to the string.

3 **Lower the bait.** Lower the bait into the water until you feel it touch the bottom.

4 **Pull up a crab.** When you feel a crab nibbling at the bait, lift it gently up and out of the water. Put the crab carefully into the bucket.

5 **Identify the crabs.** If you have different kinds of crab, see if you can identify the different species you've found.

6 **Release the crabs.** Once you've finished crabbing, carefully release the crabs back into the sea where they belong.

Try not to have too many crabs in a bucket: the crabs will not like it.

Loosely wind a bit of line around your finger. This makes it easier to feel crabs pulling on it.

Northern Kelp Crab

Dungeness Crab

King Crab

Blue Crab

Fiddler Crab

Mitten Crab

CRAB CARE!

Be careful when picking up crabs: if they pinch, it is very hard to make them let go.

Hold the crab with your finger and thumb on either side of the shell, so you don't hurt the crab. Hold it behind its pincers, so it cannot reach you with them.

21-25. Five more things . . .

Here are five more things to do outdoors. For some of them you will need help from your parents. (Usually, help with paying.)

21 **Learn to rock climb**
Many outdoor centers have rock climbing courses lasting half a day or a day.

22 **Go off-road biking**
Make sure to pick a trail that your bike can handle. Don't try to ride along a rocky, bumpy path on a road bike.

23 **Try a fun run**
In some places there are organized, timed runs around marked courses in parks and other open spaces. The courses may be 1–3 miles long. Just get an adult to register you online, turn up, and run.

24 **Set up a skateboard slalom**
All you need is a safe area, chalk to mark the start and finish lines, a stopwatch, a helmet and pads, and some cones (or old drink bottles).

25 **Read a book**
Find a quiet, comfortable spot, settle down, and concentrate on your favorite book for a while.

Index

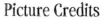

THE AUTHOR

Paul Mason is a well-known author of children's books, many award-nominated, on such subjects as how to save the planet, gross things that go wrong with the human body, and the world's craziest inventors. Many have surprising, unbelievable, or just plain disgusting facts. Today, he lives at a secret location on the coast of Europe, where his writing shack usually smells of drying wetsuit (he's a former international swimmer and an enthusiastic surfer).

Picture Credits